Disney

Miles FROM TOMORROWLAND

 phoenix international publications, inc.

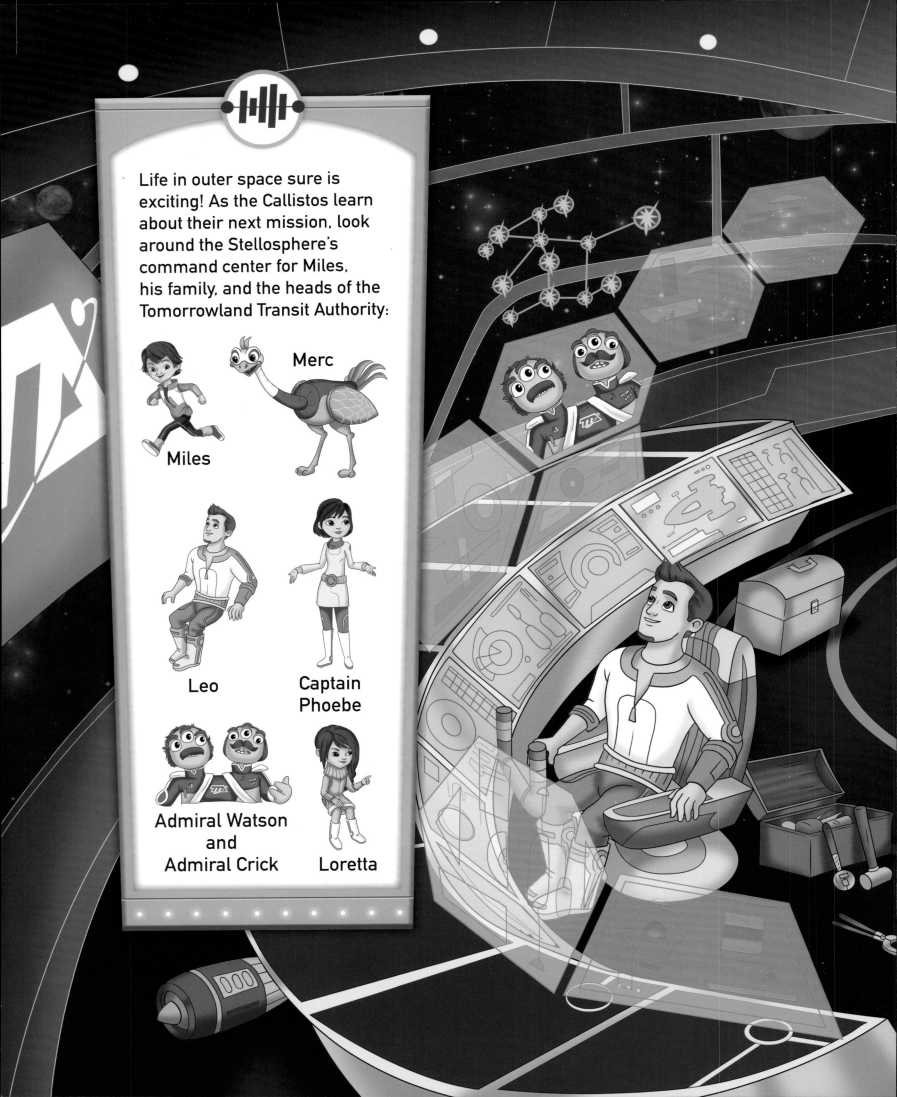

Life in outer space sure is exciting! As the Callistos learn about their next mission, look around the Stellosphere's command center for Miles, his family, and the heads of the Tomorrowland Transit Authority:

Miles

Merc

Leo

Captain Phoebe

Admiral Watson and Admiral Crick

Loretta

Sometimes the Callistos get sent on missions to *very* strange planets, like Antheia, where most of the plants are orange! While the family collects environmental samples for the Tomorrowland Transit Authority, search for these unusual living things:

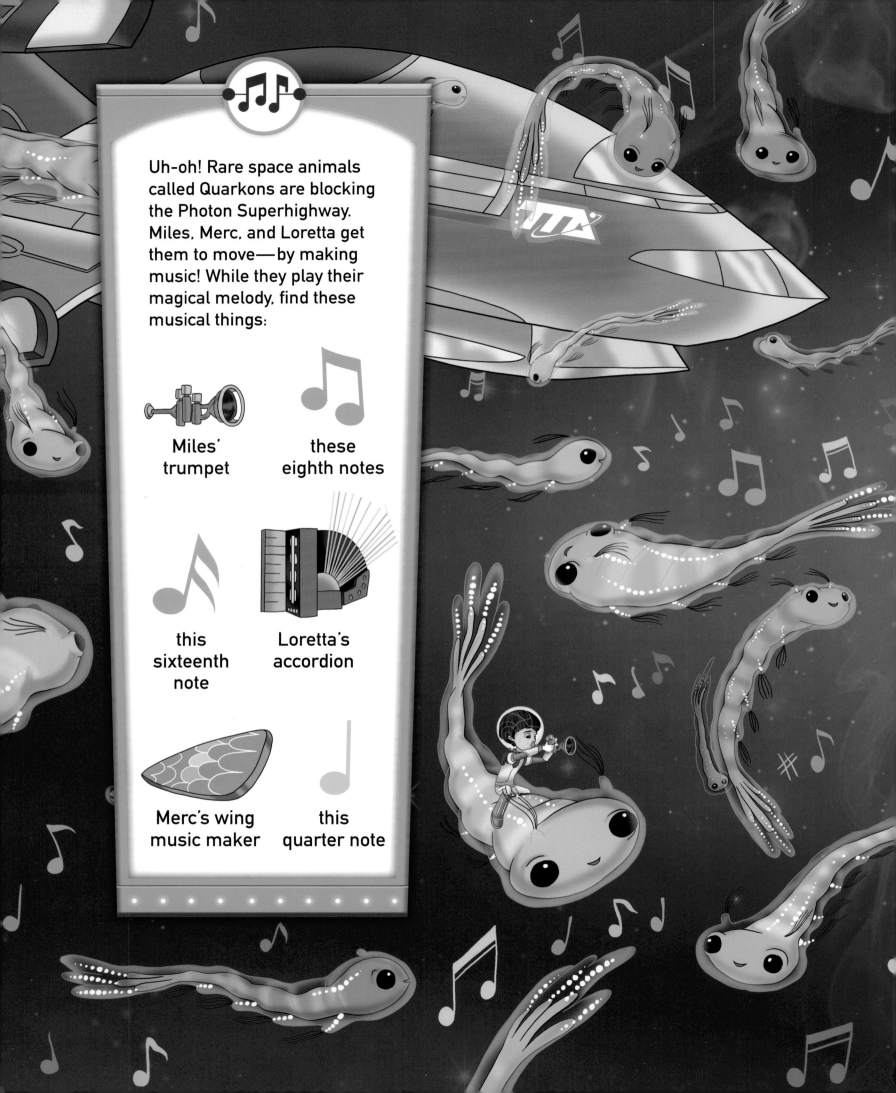

Uh-oh! Rare space animals called Quarkons are blocking the Photon Superhighway. Miles, Merc, and Loretta get them to move—by making music! While they play their magical melody, find these musical things:

Miles' trumpet

these eighth notes

this sixteenth note

Loretta's accordion

Merc's wing music maker

this quarter note

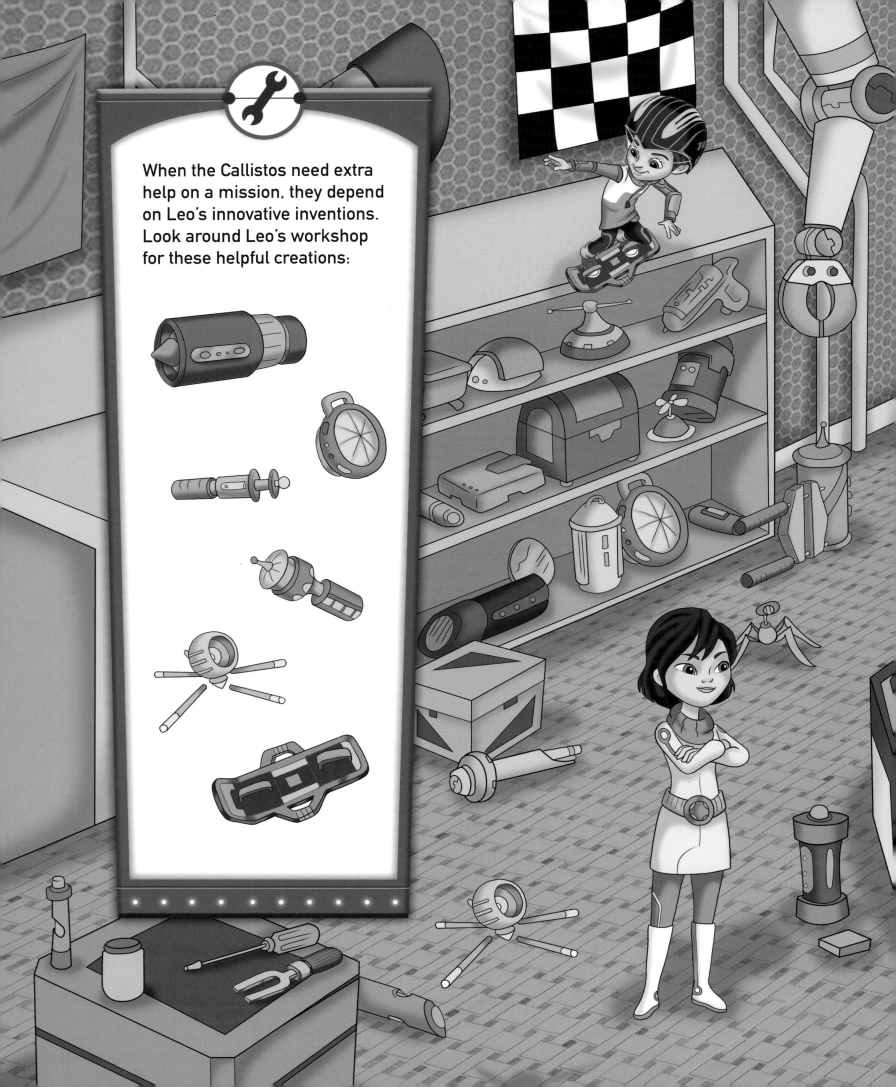

When the Callistos need extra help on a mission, they depend on Leo's innovative inventions. Look around Leo's workshop for these helpful creations:

Miles' Earth friend Haruna needs to find a new planet for his family to live on. As Miles flies the Photon Flyer, Merc tests the temperature on each planet. Can you find Merc's reactions? Which one looks just right?

Living in space has *blastastic* perks, like the Zuma Whirlpool! While Miles, Merc, and Leo ride quantum waves and surf solar wind, keep a lookout for these space rocks:

The Callistos work well together on their missions, and in their kitchen too! As they all pitch in to prepare a delicious meal, look around for these cooking tools:

this pot

tray

napkins

this pot

toaster

pitcher

In their spare time, the Callistos hang out together in their garden...that is, until Stella calls with their next mission! Quick, find these family members who are relaxing:

Loretta

Phoebe

Merc

Leo

Miles

Blast back to the command center and find these important gadgets:

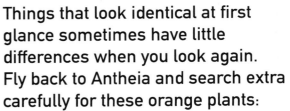

Things that look identical at first glance sometimes have little differences when you look again. Fly back to Antheia and search extra carefully for these orange plants:

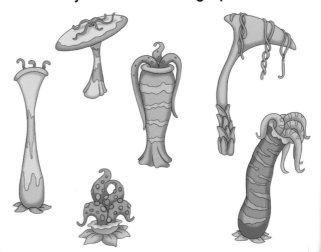

Speed back to the Photon Superhighway and look for these quirky Quarkons:

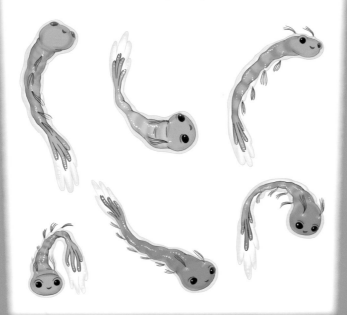

Return to Leo's workshop and find these handy tools:

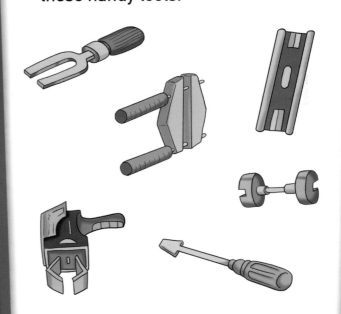

Other planets can have very different environments from Earth. Fly back to Miles and Merc's planet mission and find these conditions:

 dusty

 hot

 rainy

 foggy

 icy

 just right

Zoom back to the Zuma Whirlpool and find 3 quantum waves of each color:

 purple

 red

 pink

 yellow

 green

 orange

Living in space doesn't stop the Callistos from eating their favorite foods. Dash back to their dining room and find these dishes:

Go back to the Callistos' garden and find these things that are growing: